WOODS AND CLOUDS INTER-CHANGE-ABLE

WOODS AND CLOUDS INTERCHANGEABLE

MICHAEL EARL CRAIG

WAVE BOOKS / SEATTLE AND NEW YORK

PUBLISHED BY WAVE BOOKS

WWW.WAVEPOETRY.COM

WAVE BOOKS TITLES ARE DISTRIBUTED TO THE TRADE BY

CONSORTIUM BOOK SALES AND DISTRIBUTION

PHONE: 800-283-3572 / SAN 631-760X

LIBRARY OF CONGRESS CATALOGING-IN-PUBLICATION DATA

NAMES: CRAIG, MICHAEL EARL, AUTHOR.

TITLE: WOODS AND CLOUDS INTERCHANGEABLE /

MICHAEL EARL CRAIG.

DESCRIPTION: FIRST EDITION. | SEATTLE : WAVE BOOKS, [2019]

IDENTIFIERS: LCCN 2018032879 |

ISBN 9781940696812 (TRADE HARDCOVER)

CLASSIFICATION: LCC PS3603.R3553 A6 2019 | DDC 811/.6—DC23

LC RECORD AVAILABLE AT HTTPS://LCCN.LOC.GOV/2018032879

DESIGNED AND COMPOSED BY QUEMADURA

PRINTED IN THE UNITED STATES OF AMERICA

9 8 7 6 5 4 3 2 1

FIRST EDITION

WAVE BOOKS 076

FOR SUSAN
& FOR ODIN

A nest is a bird's house. I've known this for a long time, people have told it to me for a long time. In fact, it is such an old story that I hesitate to repeat it, even to myself.

GASTON BACHELARD

WOODS AND CLOUDS INTER- CHANGE- ABLE

WHO WAS MRS. BUTTERWORTH

Known to British
thespians as
Dame Butterworth,
a sometimes glass,
sometimes plastic
vessel into
which projections
poured. A matron
no doubt (and yet
not matronly)
who kept butter
pats beneath her
apron. Known to
her more hometown
peeps as both Joy
and Jodeen J.
Butterworth, it
was this beloved
bottle lady
who scooted a-
long our river-

banks looking for
waffles. When glass,
a gleam rose. And
when as plastic
she talked her way
into our log
homes, we sat back
and we squeezed her.

ELOISE

The room was dark.
He played roughly with his ice cream,
making quite a racket with his spoon.
We were trying to watch *Harold and Maude*
and he kept mumbling about brevity,
saying brevity was the soul of mental capability
and pragmatic resourcefulness, saying
brevity was the soul of astuteness of perception
and judgment, and that brevity was
the soul of that talent for banter and persiflage.

Now it is later,
and in a different room it is dark.
He is sleeping near me as a horse might,
on his cot. I switch a light on and
watch him. A horse cannot breathe
through its mouth. As children we'd
test this, blocking the nostrils
and waiting. A horse we all knew
would stand there looking down
his long face at us, blinking.
It was a simpler time, woods and clouds
interchangeable.

THE RABBIT

I remember the spring when the rabbit with no ears showed up.
Little pink stubs.
Were they bleeding?
Had they been ripped or chewed off?
This rabbit hopped about and enjoyed eating grass no differently.
At first it was unsettling, then amusing, then normal.
Then company would come and say look at that rabbit!
And it would again seem odd, unsettling, but eventually normal.

The ears were not there but not bleeding.
It gave the helmet effect.
And we ran.
We ran from this rabbit.
Although it was only me.
Always only me on the porch.
Running through the ages from this casual rabbit.
Who enjoyed the grass no differently.

HOW TO FIX A BROKEN
BUTTERFLY WING

Alice I thought you'd want to see this.
It's over nine minutes long but worth it.
I am your uncle and not a butterfly expert
but still it looks legit.

Ten items are needed:

       —old towel

       —wire hanger

       —toothpicks

       —Q-tips

       —new wings

       —tweezers

       —baby powder

       —scissors

       —contact adhesive

       —cardstock

This is a cooperative butterfly.
Not all butterflies are like this.

He might even be sedated.
Sedation is typically administered
by carefully blowing
a little puff of laughing gas
directly into the face of a butterfly.

To immobilize your patient
you basically grab him.
And we're in a dimly lit room
to keep him calm.
And remember glue is permanent!

So go to your pile of used wings,
hopefully you've collected some.
Match up the veins.
Don't glue him to the towel.
And finish with some baby powder.

Near the end comes a somber warning:

DO NOT BURDEN YOUR FRIEND
WITH LARGE ADDITIONS.
PRACTICE BEFORE IF POSSIBLE.

But Alice in order to practice
you will need another butterfly.

WHO WAS VERONICA

Friends called her a
saint and maybe
so did Jesus
as he stopped to
smell the gravel.
In truth she worked
at the local
laundromat fold-
ing towels and
daily bleaching
things like bibs and
the then-trendy
beard protectors
seen all over
Jerusalem.
Veronica
is not mentioned
in the Bible
but her veil went
viral causing
copies of all

kinds to be made.
Fakes! Fakes! is what
the by the way
thick-bearded Pope
Paul the Fifth said
(1616)
and he banned that
lucrative job—
though the Vati-
can kept safe theirs.

TOWN

Town was holding its annual pageant
down by the river.
Floats and kettle corn.
Clowns, horns, stuff like that.
The first float came into view.
Not really a float.
It was a men's plaid sport coat
just floating down the river toward us
facedown with arms akimbo.
It rippled noiselessly past us.
For a few minutes nothing happened.
Then came the Shriners, swimming in
white underwear. Hats above water.
Yelping. Struggling. A couple of them
disappeared beneath the surface.
Then it was quiet. Nothing happened.
Probably five minutes passed.
Then a homemade-looking raft
with a slippery-looking hog on it
came into view. The hog was covered
with brown spots. "Leeches!"

someone shouted. People laughed.
Not everyone. No one was sure.
"It's a greased hog on a raft with
maybe leeches," someone said.
"It's not grease," someone said.
"It's maybe sunscreen," someone said.
"Those leeches aren't biting," said a man
holding a stiff slice of pizza.
The river sparkled. Big trucks moved
ant-like up a mountain in the distance,
belching blue puffs. "If those are leeches,"
said a young mother holding her baby,
"I say they're friendly leeches."
"Leeches ain't always evil," said another.
Then the baby who was maybe six months old said
"Opportunistic leeches."
He blinked, working his fingers.
"That's our greased hog."
His voice was deep and calm.
"Covered with opportunistic leeches."

YOU SHOULD BE HEARING THE
SOUND THAT A MARBLE MAKES

There is a blue marble rolling slowly toward you.
A large blue marble that can roll uphill.
Slowly over books.
Or a pile of laundry.
Doing a "load of socks."

DIMES

We destroyed the banana, peeling it.
There was a white witch.
The white witch drove a dark Prius.
Dimes dropped from a passing helicopter
were just beginning to hit the deep snow.

At the end of a trying life it's comforting
to watch a dog drink water.
It's somehow gratifying to watch plants
get watered.
To see water pour into a plant
and darken the soil and disappear.

Each dime hits and penetrates the snow like a wink.
A noiseless blip.
Dimes, being dropped from a helicopter.
Disappearing into the snow.

WHO WAS PONTIUS PILATE

A compulsive
handwasher who
could wear khakis
with khaki smocks
and beige sandals.
Homely. A fat
nose some say while
others step up
to say nose was
more or less right.
A suicide,
his body tossed
in the Tiber—
it floated. Then
hucked in the Rhône—
again rose. So
it was off then
to some lake, some
lake near Lucerne,
site of endless
agitations.

THE QUALITY OF LIGHT

1

The other idiot was found in a meadow the color of biscuits. The light was warm and round and a little coppery.

2

We approached this other idiot slowly, with exterior caution. On the insides we were rushing I suppose, flapping our arms.

3

Who *we* was is (or maybe isn't) somewhat complicated. It was me and Christian and Rhoda.

4

The light had chocolate notes with hints of salted peanuts and banana bread.

5

Of caramel and geraniums, a little tobacco, and white pepper.

6

The other idiot sat in a chair in the meadow. No, he sat on the ground, hugging his knees and rocking. No, he sat in a chair.

7

The story starts, it always does, with something that happened earlier, it always does.

8

And moving away from all that is essential, really, and so I'm asking you please to reconsider your stance.

9

Oh and you can't just go rushing up to the other idiot. He/she might be in a chair or down on the ground rocking and hugging his/her knees.

10

Cannot just go rushing into a meadow the color of biscuits.

11

You are there to take stock. To record. To comment on the light. The quality of light.

12

Be sure to take notes on the quality of light.

JOCELYN

A cat has jumped in through an open window
and knocked the chimera embryos from their beaker.

A cat's just jumped in through a window knocking
embryos onto the counter.

Onto the counter it's chimeric embryos thanks
to the cat who has jumped.

A left-open window for a cat to come through,
bumping a beaker.

FROM BED

The wind is howling. But also mewling.
Ornate wicker feelings rip loose
and tear off down valley.
Cabin: half buried in snow.
Bedsprings: if I were *dead* these would still creak.
Blankets: could use another.
A bruised light through lace curtains,
maybe a baby's finger of bourbon in the bottle.

Something small's just run
across me, diagonally,
across chest and stopped
on stomach, panting.
Kneading his or her paws a bit
on the topmost, pilly, filthy, beware
of adjectives blanket. Ripped
loose wicker feelings traveling
back now, up valley.

WHO WAS KING FRIDAY

The oaken son
of King Charming
Thursday and Queen
Cinderella
Monday, infant
Friday was born
with real teeth in
his head. Began
attending the
Kingly School when
just six months old.
Siblings Paul and
Celeste. Pet birds
(also oaken)
(and on long sticks)
Mimus Poly-
glottos and Trog-
lodytes Aedon.
A ruler kept
when not in use
in a cardboard

box with balsam
wife Queen Sara
Saturday and
their Bakelite
child Prince Tuesday.
Despite being
wooden Friday'd
cut himself each
day at dawn with
his razor while
shaving his legs,
a foot propped at
sink's edge. "My close
friend Crimson Drop-
let I presume?"
is how each time
he would greet blood
in the basin.
For Friday had
flair. Was at one
time a Mason.

COLOSSEUM

I am sitting in a café with my right hand up to my face.
My hand smells like fresh laundry.
I watch a muffin go by. A baby swats
with his fist, dumping a lemonade.
I have a hand to my face and it smells like fresh laundry.
Someone's grandma is covered in new green-blue tattoos.
There is the sadness of unwed despots,
the chromed anger of the espresso nozzle,
a man with what looks like potatoes in his pants—
one in the front and one in the back.
People are squirting sriracha onto everything.
People, squirting sriracha onto everything.

THE PROBLEM

The insect said
to the rabbit
the problem is
I know who my
heroes are and
I know who your
heroes are. You
only know who
your heroes are.
What? said rabbit.
You don't even
know what kind of
insect I am
said the insect.
What? said rabbit.

CHUNK OF SEA GLASS

Becky I'm typing this in your study.
It's a rainy fall day and for some reason
I want to type "you're in Japan" and
don't know where your man and kid are.
Man and kid feels a little crass but
it's okay because I've let myself into
your house and I'm weak, and drunk, and
a little hungry, looking at a sizable chunk
of blue-green sea glass here on your desk,
considering the weight it exerts upon the desk
and the desk's equal (inverse) force upon its base.

A thunderstorm's just passed through,
I type that. And one of your windows
is cracked slightly—the study sips the balmy
air. The room smells like old books.
There's a red wig on a wig rack,
a heavy black stapler that feels like a pistol,
a water glass with an inch of water in it.

Soon Becky I will recline in your recliner,
your cat sprawled on my abdomen,
making it difficult to nap. But I'll nap.
And when I wake I'll still have the house
to myself I am sure. And all the browns
and beiges and burnt mustards of your study
will resume again their quiet work on me,
coaxing me along on my journey without you
(who may or may not be in Japan), your man
or your kid.

WHO WAS THE SUN

Before the Sun
was the Sun
the Sun was
other things.
Used-car salesman.
Bible salesman.
Door-to-door
gourd salesman.
Circus employee.
Early orthodontist.
Warrior. Witch.
Black hole.
Wind in the grass.
Snake in the grass.
Then car salesman
again. That was
eons ago.
Then the Sun
became the Sun,
our great enabler.
Endurance personified.

Witness. Savior.
Silent partner.
Savage, stoic, cynic.
The Sun partied,
was a talker,
grew weary,
made a comeback,
had a heyday,
then lost traction,
again grew weary—
used cars, gourds, Bibles.

THE COUPLE

She threw her Thomas Bernhard books at him,
it took eight or nine minutes.
Then she left, running over him with her Yukon.
The cigarette she'd thrown down
smoked itself without fanfare
in the crushed gravel of the footpath.

My binoculars make a small gap in the living room curtains.

He rolls over in the drive, onto his back,
and tries to wiggle his toes, but cannot.
Oh the day does darkle, he thinks . . .
right away wondering about his use of darkle.
But the day *is* darkling.
Oh yes indeed, indubitably it darkles.

GIANT HOTEL FERN

It's said that when it's time for coffee
and a roll, head straight for the fern
and make a hard left.

When it's a morning paper you're after
go toward the fern, bear right, stay
close to the fern, rounding it—
look for Exit 232.

This is a giant fern and people
are streaming early into the glorious lobby,
some of them barefoot,
in white robes searching
for coffee, for rolls, for newsprint.

It's said that this fern is at the center of Rome.
Maybe twelve feet wide and with a breeze inside.

It's said that Rome is the greatest city for walking
but when I check it's in eleventh place.

It's said that if a white, plain-looking, thick
book called *What Is Poetry?* falls
with a thump
onto a table before you,
don't open it.

DON CHEADLE POEM

I've been working on my Don Cheadle poem
for hours now and nothing's happening.
I am at home, working on my Don Cheadle poem.
My Don Cheadle poem seemed like a good idea
earlier, but not so much now. Nothing interests me
in my Don Cheadle poem. If I knew how to get
my Don Cheadle poem off the ground I
would do that.

WHO WAS CATULLUS

Libidinous
comet savant
traveling some-
times at us with
simpering boy-
tools on tethers.
Fresh lettuce hung
from his rafters.
Au revoir (?) he'd
say, waving scarf
and/or crumpet.
Spread himself thin.
(He didn't mind.)
So many oth-
er people's gar-
dens to tend to—
invectives and
condolences—
his married girl-
friend, Clodia.

Could be Caesar
would want his pool
cleaned. Thoroughly.
All gates left a-
jar in autumn.

AT THE PARTY

No one noticed when I backed out of the room
and went downstairs into the basement and found
under an air hockey table a dollhouse and got down
on hands and knees and crawled toward it
and put my left eye up to one of the windows
and tried looking in, feeling the cool air that
was in there brush my eye, making my eye feel dry.
I thought maybe I sensed the presence of a couple
of well-made wooden chairs in there, that was all—
one of them up against a wall and one tipped over in
the middle of the floor.

THIS LOOKS RUSSIAN TO ME

It's a postcard of a painting of a man and a dead woman.
A waterfront scene. The man is large and sits smoking, casually.
The woman is dead, or maybe sleeping, but probably dead,
and laid out flat on her back, in black, with black hair
poured out like seaweed on the sand around her head.

It's an old card, no information on the back. The man sits
on the edge of a beached rowboat smoking a pipe, watching us.
A wisp of smoke takes off from the side of his face and travels away.
The woman's eyes are closed. She looks waterlogged. A long
black dress clings to her body. She wears lace-up ankle boots
with heels. She is definitely dead.

Although maybe they're thespians taking turns pretending
to be dead. It is the woman's turn and so she's down now
on her back in the sand at the water's edge, and it's the man
who's just taken her pipe and gone and sat on the boat's edge.
He needed a match. She handed one up to him. Moving only
her left arm to do so. Shoulders down flat on the sand so as not
to mess her hair, which the man had just carefully arranged
like a bouquet about her head.

In the distance there's a faint skyline of buildings—the suggestion
of just the tips of spires in the fog. The man wears old boots
and multiple capes or cloaks of wool and canvas, and a kind of
military cap with a short bill. He is probably a policeman, a
    constable,
and looks neither shocked nor bored. Not tired and yet resting.
He has seen it all before. He is permitting us to take it all in.

At the woman's heels we see what might be drag marks in the
    sand.
Behind her where the water starts is a flimsy dock of planks
of varying lengths and qualities. A single crow is walking or
    standing
here, stooping. If birds used canes he would definitely have one.
He is tiny in this painting, a little flourish, but full of feeling and
    purpose.
He is Russian like the others. And exists to draw the eye.

WHAT BUGGED ME WAS

how they had you
in your casket with
one arm tucked
behind your head.
It looked too final.
It seemed redundant.

WHO WAS FRANZ LISZT

Preferred haircuts:
the striking "Dutch
Nun"—a.k.a.
"The Spaniel"—and
his signature
"Curtains" (blown dry).
Plagued, it's pointed
out often, by
dropsy, asthma,
insomnia,
a cataract,
and heart disease,
not to mention
his feelings of
desolation.
You can hear it
in his music.
His pedaling
said to be a
form of breathing.
His breathing said

to be strangely
similar to
his use of the
pedals. Father
of Cosima,
who was married
to von Bülow
but ran off with
Wagner, who's said
to've gone on to
woo someone named
Gautier and
perhaps even
Pringle, do you
follow? [faint creak-
ing of pedals]
Gradually
winter rolled in.

SOME TEA HAS EVAPORATED HERE

Two clouds cast shadows on
the lumpy mountain. The shadows
move like amoebas.
Like moods. Stains. No, moods.

I thought I might want to write awhile
about the Augean stables. I felt I
wanted to make some connections, draw
some parallels.

Instead I'm looking down
into my teacup at
the brown residue that
was recently tea.

A cloud inks the mountain briefly.
A shadow rippling over pine trees.
It is Saturday.
I hold out my finger for a monarch.

YOUR PAINTING

When I step toward this
I hear a hatchet
hatcheting—
crack (pause) *crack* (pause)
crack—

and lemonade spurts
from a trunk weirdly
where we'd felt
something else might
ooze.

Metallic taste of lilac
lacing the air,
lips dusted with
pheromones,
gums tingling,
and a kind of
fruit-sense
matting the grass.

At the picnic
there's a chair
we make Uncle
sit in, although he
does not want to.

And as I step
toward this,
your painting,
I'm met with
EYES,
a gentle buzz
in the earth,
smell of clipped mint,
sound of mowers
gagging lazily on
wet wads,
and a late snake
making her way
unharmed in the grass
I have mentioned.

At the picnic is a chair
in which Uncle sits,
cracking a cold one,
his interest in tomorrow.

THE TURIN HORSE

Ricsi is an actor, known for The Turin Horse *(2011)*

—*IMDb*

After leading a typical horse life
and having some tough stretches
of neglect, as horses sometimes do,
Ricsi lands the lead in Béla Tarr's
The Turin Horse.

She plays the farmer's horse.
She has a deep sadness in her eyes,
dislikes moving with a carriage.

Tarr has to find an actor to play the farmer
who can work well with Ricsi.
Someone Ricsi wants to work with.

The farmer is played by János Derzsi,
best known for *Werckmeister Harmonies* (2000)
and *Satantango* (1994).

Erika Bók plays the farmer's daughter.
She's best known for roles in
The Man from London (2007)
and *Satantango*.

The only other actor in Tarr's film is Mihály Kormos
(*The Man from London*, *Werckmeister Harmonies*, *Satantango*)
who plays a babbling Nietzschean visitor
who stops in for a drink and a monologue.

The film is narrated by Mihály Ráday,
cinematographer and actor,
and son of actor Imre Ráday.

Wind and boiled potatoes feature prominently.

Tarr and his cinematographer never discussed Nietzsche.
It was not necessary.

WHO WAS SIMONE WEIL

Supposedly
a mentor she
admired called her
the Red Virgin.
And The Martian.
Both compliments.
Her hands were small.
Much too small for
her body her
mom felt. Sometimes
writing less is
okay. Is best.

BILLINGS CLINIC, ROOM 2508

When it's time to take a leak you'll need to get up, move the awkward table on wheels to the left, push the vinyl recliner to the right, and drag your IV caddy with you into the bathroom. (Where are your slippers?) In order to step into the bathroom you will need to push the plastic shower stool over toward the toilet. Once you're in the bathroom with the door shut, the plastic shower stool needs to go somewhere else, like behind you, where it will block the door in a minute when you're trying to leave. To get out, move the plastic shower stool, open the door, step into the room, go toward the bed dragging IV caddy, and pull the awkward table in behind you so that once you're in bed you'll be able to reach it. The recliner can stay where it is but someone will come in soon and need to move it. They will move it your way so they can get to their computer station, and in doing so they will block you in. If you need to get to the sink, get up and begin moving everything in the other direction. (Where are your slippers?) You won't get to the sink—or to the window, or to the closet—without moving the awkward table on wheels to the right, back into the center of the room, and in order to do that the big vinyl recliner can't be there, but most likely it is.

IDEAS FOR A MOSTLY SILENT FILM
IN THREE FIFTEEN-MINUTE SCENES

The new veterinarian had come at me
with his rubber bucket of whip-its,
exiting bumpily the field
over clod and stubble. A swather
swathed with a clank and a rattle.
A young boy with enormous weathered hands
shoveled silage machinelike.
He moved his hands like heavy paddles,
swatting occasionally at a hummingbird.

Across the field was another field
and across that field the farmhouse
with farm fresh eggs on (I bet)
the counter, and real farm blankets
in six different languages, on each
of the beds, in each of the bedrooms.
A not-quite-toothless man in a fresh diaper
lit a match to light a cigar—it
went out. He lit another. It went out.

A giant airship moved very slowly
overhead, with Waldorf salads, we'd
read, served on board. Smoke leaked
from a hole in its side. And it
occurred to me then that, seasonally,
silage and hummingbirds together
don't go. Which of course caused
our sweaters to unravel. The air
tasting of grapes. And walnuts.

GENTLY TAPPING RAVIOLIS
IN A POT OF BOILING WATER

31 December 2016

It is New Year's
and a poet is stirring raviolis
made by his portfolio manager,
using an impressive wooden spoon
carved by another poet.
(A long, narrow package had arrived in the mail.)

Lots of comments on
the way a tapped ravioli gives
a little, and sinks down for
just a second . . .

We feel refreshed, watching.
We feel rinsed.
It is the end of a very odd year.

A very odd year is finally coming to a close.

WHO WAS MAN O' WAR

A coiled spring, son
of Fair Play, great
grandfather to
renowned Swaps, the
"California
Cripple." Known when
young to scream with
rage, to sometimes
dump wan jockey—
his favorite treat
a chilled orange.
It's said he "grieved
himself to death,"
age thirty. Re-
quired twenty-three
bottles of em-
balming fluid.
Lay in state for
two days, with fans
from world over
streaming slowly

past him in dark
veils, fedoras,
starched ensembles,
smell of mothballs.
In the photos
these people look
equally dead.
Was it winter?
Heavily clothed
toddlers sit on
the edge of the
moat, shoes dangling.

FINDINGS

The umlaut was almost nonexistent in 1800.
Began to lift its sleepy head a bit in 1820.
Crept along with ups and downs.
Really hopped between 1876 and 1890.
The early 1960s showed even more progress.
Peaked in 1975.
Tanked in '85.
Spiked again in '92.
Tanking again, though, now.
Why?

ICE, SALAD, GLOVES

I pick up the puppy and go through the house,
introducing him to it.
This is the brown chair (I tip him toward it).
This is the lamp (I tip him toward it).
Just look at this lampshade (I re-tip him).
This is the old clock (I tip him toward it).
Ticktock the old clock, I say.
He looks at it.
Here are some slippers (I kick them)
We move on to the kitchen.
Nuts. Limes. Gin.
The potted amaryllis (a long tip).
His eyes move from the amaryllis to the cheese.
Cheese, I say, tipping him.
Ice. Salad. Gloves.

NATALIA

Natalia had left some seeds uneaten; it was unlike her.
She was banging her beak on the bars of her cage.
A real wolf in sheep's clothing said the chimney sweep,
eyeing her with caution. He had a powerful vacuum
which he maneuvered unnecessarily near her.
He had numerous tarps down, and a cup of tea,
and a filthy boom box . . . some Nina Simone . . .
"Who Knows Where the Time Goes."
Natalia buried her beak beneath her wing.
She listened.

WHO WAS FRÄULEIN UNBEKANNT

A German with
perhaps a slight
Russian accent.
Had sixty cats.
Jumped from a bridge
in Berlin once—
from the Bendler-
brücke into the
Landwehrkanal.
And oh, right, was
thought to be the
lost Grand Duchess
Anastasia.
An impostor?
Maybe. About
five out of ten
people believed.
Her nostrils looked
different—so
said her old math
tutor. Her star

was bright but soon
tilted. Wilted?
All sixty cats
put to death in
a town called Un-
terlengenhardt.
Five out of ten.
Not bad if you
think about it.

THE CHANGE

With concern for the country
we've just lacquered two stools,

now I'm in the back yard
squirtin' down the new mule.

You're in the sacristy
with a gentle ragout.

Regarding such lacquers
you say you've no clue.

I turn slowly in space
like a galvanized screw,

turning ever so slowly
in concepts of blue.

Your pace is more quick
like a well-handled tool.

We trade thoughts without speaking.
Our seams tear without leaking.

The bedroom is squeaking
(not my mother's canoe).

The bedroom is barking.
Mental snow, on my shoes.

ROSE TANTRUM

A rose was throwing a tantrum
deep in the botanical gardens.
An angel fell in the bathroom,
knocked her front teeth out
on the edge of the toilet.
A long-haired dachshund was
crossing the Bosporus I'm
jumping around here. A rose.
A tantrum. An angel saying
it was the sink. A sign
on a dumpster saying
UNWANTED DIAMONDS.
But it was the toilet.
Was definitely the toilet.

The rose shook slightly
but violently. Like a bruise
happening. Sound of cable
straining. The angel danced
all night in a club. Music
deafening. Rum & Cokes.

Carpenter blokes. Dried
blood on her chin. I fell
and smashed these in
she tried saying, pointing
to her mouth. On the sink!
Today! At noon! The sink!

THANKSGIVING

I will have fallen deeply asleep
flat on my back
in the middle of the living room floor

with a damp washcloth over my face
when the company arrives
streaming into the room

with cold air in their clothes and hair.
And one of them will come
quietly over to me

I will later be told
and touch my temple gently with
her boot.

WHO WAS HIERONYMUS BOSCH

Or what about
Roscoe Conkling?
I lie down at
the foot of his
statue—sit up
only to give
his bronze boot a
lick. A lawyer-
bodybuilder
who chased women
and liked to box
and who in youth
kept tucked it's told
The Art of Speak-
ing, The Art of
Speaking, The Art
of Speaking, The
Art of Speaking
beneath his arm.

NPR

The doctors were cutting a man's head off.
We could hear this on the radio.
I said, "Wait."
And, "That sounds like some kind of *saw*."
"That's a chainsaw," you said.
We were eating dinner.
At which point they said, "The
sound you're hearing is that
of the Milwaukee 12 amp Sawzall."
They had to work quickly.
The idea was to cut the man's head off
carefully, and then turn and somehow
sew it onto the other man's body.
So two heads were coming off.
One was bad and the other was good.
If all went well then the good head
they explained could be paired with
the good body, and go on to enjoy a full life.
The bad head and body could be discarded.

THE BRANCHES OF CLOWNS

The avenging clown sat at the table in his underwear.
Vana Kloun was his stage name.
The avenging clown slumped forward and made a noise
into his porridge. It was dark out.
An almost inaudible noise that only the dogs could hear,
who slunk to the farthest corners of the room.
The avenging clown had smeared his makeup,
had taken the back of his hand and smeared his makeup,
emitting a sound only the dogs could hear.

In the park the avenging clown dragged each foot
as one might drag a washing machine.
First the one, then the other. Then the one
and again the other. This went on all morning,
the dogs loose and trailing their leashes,
peeing on rocks, chasing squirrels.

At the mall the avenging clown fell down
the empty escalator, banging his head really hard
a number of times, all the while holding
a cup of hot coffee. Adrian who is an expert on

clown behavior will say this stanza gets
"a little too slapstick." And so we talk about it,
and decide that it doesn't.

At home the avenging clown slumped again
at the kitchen table. It was dark out. Besides
avenging clowns you have reductive clowns,
motorcycle-cop clowns, contemplative clowns,
and sozzled clowns. And child-prodigy clowns.
And adult-onset clowns. And also your standard
anguished clowns. These are the primary
branches of clowns I'm aware of.

MARYLAND

When I threw that Chapstick down
onto the comforter it
sent ripples through
Maryland.

WHO WAS CHIEF PLENTY COUPS

Considered the
last of the great
Apsáalooke chiefs,
the last Crow chief
elected by
other chiefs, a
real chief's chief who
carried a pair
of chickadee
legs in a small
medicine bag
and could wear a
wolf's head over
his own and go
drinking milk at
night from his neigh-
bor's fridge. Sometimes
seen in a black
suit coat with stiff
cuffed black jeans, a
nine-gallon cream-

color Stetson,
gold spectacles
(circular), and
pencil-thin braids
down both sides of
his head like an-
tennae. When he
moved or blinked you
could see beams of
turquoise light flash
from tiny holes
in his shirt and
from the cuffs of
his dark jacket.
Born at a place
called *The-cliff-that
has-no-pass*. It's
gone from there now.

THE SIGNAL

You say the manuscript is in the mail.
I say the condor has no voice box.
You say the flour is in the soufflé.
I say the gloved hand holds the red crumb.
You say the egg is in the army helmet.
I say the chin strap has been weakened.

We look at each other.

The bored baby soils his swaddle.
The narwhal is retreating.

28 APRIL 2016

When you were dying
people talked about you
in the past tense which
I found annoying.

Now that you have died
people refer to you in
the present tense which
I also am struggling with.

I'M IN ROOM 927

With thumb and forefinger I examined the ball-peen hammer.
The sparrow slid violently into third base.
Night after night it was NASCAR, kettle corn, karaoke.
Wendy wore burlap, clapping her hands.
Zinc divided the men from the boys.
My mind made a snuffling noise.
The forest absorbed us, knowing all along.
Peg slid her girlhood toward us across the ages.
When I say indigo bunting I fucking mean indigo bunting.
The kiln was a metaphor Joan was fond of.
The greased hog loved the attention.
The orphan snapped me in the groin with his towel.

*

The lump in Jim's pants was his ball-peen hammer.
The sparrow was a piece of meat with wings.
Night laid us all face down in the grass and "flossed" us.
Wearing burlap Wendy stepped into the phone booth.
Bradley had a funny little zinc limp.
My mind drank from its tank.
The forest was full of gongs.
Girlhood, down the chimney.

Did I not say indigo bunting?
Joan talked on and on about the kiln, gesturing.
I stood at attention, which many felt unnecessary.
The orphan recommended the steak tartare.

*

The ball-peen hammer was spending the century at the bottom of
    Lake Baikal.
The sparrow swept crumbs with one wing, slapped at the cat with
    the other.
Night with a little spit on its chin.
Wendy allowed herself to be shot from a cannon (wearing burlap).
It was zinc that they found in our long johns.
My mind undressed itself a little.
Don't believe what you're told in a forest.
Girlhood tore the month of May a new one.
Kurt stepped a little too honestly toward us from his robe of indigo
    bunting.
We'd decided the kiln had a soft spot, and searched for it.
You suggested I pay attention.
I cried out to the orphan. To all orphans.

*

With pigeon shit from the '80s the ball-peen hammer'd been
    carefully caked.
The sparrow was walleyed; he looked at Denise coldly.

Night was crawling toward me like some kind of injured kitten.

If it looks, feels, and smells like burlap it still could be canvas.

The counter was made of zinc; the gerbil sensed this.

My mind kicked twice at the stall wall.

Jim moved into his closet as if it were a forest.

The chapter on girlhood upset us.

All the November babies were covered with indigo buntings.

I set my beer on Joan's kiln and she smacked me.

Attention, waning.

The nightjar was an orphan, and sat in the highest branches.

*

After rewinding, the police watched again what Eileen's eyes did
as she said *bull-peen hammer*.

The sparrow ate pulled pork for fifty minutes.

Night foamed at the mouth—not good.

They say Christ wore both socks and a shoulder bag made of burlap.

We ran through the museum sucking zinc lozenges.

A low voice said *you have broken my mind* into an omelet.

When they slit open the unicorn it was full of forests.

Girlhood stopped the mowers that were idling in the lilac.

I ask to have only indigo bunting pulled over my eyes.

The kiln is loose now, and alone, and rolls unsteadily across town.

Now Jim will demonstrate what heightened attention looks like.

The orphan could only play the Liszt sonatas with a paper bag over
her head.

WHO WAS JOAN OF ARC

A pious child,
grave beyond her
years, wore a plaid
cloak, thick glasses,
her friends called her
Joanie of Arc.
History feared
her. She said she
heard Voices. She
said she saw Lights.
Had a dachshund
she called Kenny.
She slept always
fully dressed, her
parents the re-
tiring type. It's
believed there were
more than one of
her. Unlike the
rest of us she
had just one ex-

ecutioner.

His name was Geoff

Thérage. They say

he paused. But this

ain't about him.

LADY CHAMBLESS'S YARD

Looking yesterday upstream
I saw floating toward me
a mitten beagle down

down the Shields River
bobbing, treading water
with what appeared to be

a very French expression on
his face although
it couldn't have possibly

been that—
moving diagonally across
the river's surface

to get to a spot in the bank
where he exited flawlessly
up onto a log and shook himself

a bit without stopping
and made a sharp turn
onto a wide plank

which had him trotting
across then the river into
Lady Chambless's yard.

THE DEAD ELEPHANT

1

I remember feeling it was ridiculous,
my watching him watch through binoculars
a dead elephant for maybe forty minutes.
He had asked me to remain in the Jeep.
I remember at the time I felt outraged.
When in reality I might've just been upset.
It's difficult now to separate what was
happening then, what I was really feeling,
from how I've come to talk about it.
It was a summer of portentous metaphors.
Nothing was simply what it was.
Everything meant something else.
For example this dead elephant.
I think it was 1967. It was hot out.
The mud had its cracks. The cicadas, loud.

2

When it was my turn I crawled out from the bush
and walked slowly toward it. It's difficult now
to separate what was happening then, what I
was really feeling, from how I've come to talk
about it, and it was hot out, the mud had cracks

in it, and I remember how loud the cicadas were.
And something stank. Probably the elephant
I remember thinking. And when I got there
I respectfully reached out with my stick
and I poked it.

The stick made a depression in the skin,
the skin which looked like bark, and when
I removed the stick the depression stayed.
It was the summer I first tasted whiskey.
The summer I'd dreamt every night
of seeing an elephant.

3

Way out across the valley floor I saw
a dark mound. Through binoculars
it became an elephant, dead, for sure,
for there was a boy with a stick who
was standing there poking it. It's difficult
now to separate what was happening then,
what I was really feeling, from how I've
come to talk about it, it was so hot out,
the mud had cracks in it, and I
remember how loud the cicadas were.

My guess is the summer of '68. I'd no
idea who Janis Joplin was. Or the Stones.
Or Martin Buber. Why do you ask?

THE DROPKICK

A hurricane wept through a wasteland.
No number of Kleenexes could've sopped it.
A man (hands cologned) considered
documenting this, exhuming his blue
camera from mothballs. Instead he

drop-kicked an orange through
the town's only goalposts.
The kicked orange was spectacular—
no one saw where it landed.
Mother watched it all through a part

in our living room curtains.
She said the man limped. And that
his legs stiffened as the rocks
beneath his feet began to cry.
To cry? I asked.

To cry, she said.
Now he's climbing up on a cross, she said.
A big wooden cross on the hill, she said.
Mother always called a spade a spade.
Me, not so much.

WHO WAS LU YOU

Lu You was
one of those guys
toward whom streams
ran. He had un-
usually steady
hands. Was one
shrewd business-
man. Traded
rice crackers for
bear hugs. Sold
gun smoke in
his grocery store—
came vacuum-
packed in hand-
blown blue glass.
(5 year warranty)

THE FAIR

The day had passed.
It was how we knew
the fair was over.

A somber saint marked
my head with ash.

The fields were green.
The clover hissed.
The crowd got gassed.
The air then burst
with rainbow mist.

Fresh coats of paint.
You showed restraint.
I've no complaint.
Though do feel super shaky.

For the fields were green.
The clover hissed.
The crowd got gassed.
The air then burst
with rainbow mist.

HOW I SPENT THE AFTERNOON

(a)

When driving nails into a casket
look down through the nail.

See through its center the long nail
to sort of throw the hammer through.

It seems we're under the impression
we're somehow beyond nailing
up caskets.

(b)

I'm over at the glass cabinet
taking down the notebook, the chalk
pencils, a couple of beakers—

the tall slender one as well as
the taller more slender one.

It's how I spent the afternoon.

CURRENTLY OVER KANSAS

You'd smashed a fairly
expensive painting
over my head.
You were not mad,
said not a word.
I sat there with
my oatmeal before me.
Head poking through
canvas. Frame down
around shoulders.

I'm traveling across
this great country
sideways, five or six feet
above the ground,
probably 75 m.p.h.—
legs just dangling,
not bumping into
anything—wearing only
a windbreaker.

WHO WAS SIR ERNEST HENRY SHACKLETON

An infant born
slightly sunburnt
with wide coarse beard
and half-inch-thick
sweater-vest in
sky-blue boiled wool.
Right from the chute
had a penchant
for whale blubber.
Routinely said
"A live donkey
is better than
a dead lion."
Would watch fellow
classmates at school
through a long brass
telescope. Smelled
of cologne but
never wore it.

TWO PEOPLE

We'll be like two people on different trains
who at one point cross paths on foot in a train yard
before getting back on different trains. Two people
at a salad bar, on opposite sides of a salad bar, reaching
with tongs (the cornichons) and looking through—
at but not seeing each other. Two flames moving up
a wooden Ferris wheel. A steak and a steak knife
that have no fork or candles.

HOTEL FINLEN

My pasty barked
when I cut into it.

Big trucks banged
the dumpsters.

Seemed actually
to hump them.

That was earlier.
Now a white slice

of hall light
from under the

closed door.
And somewhere

in the dark
on the bureau

the chained saint
Christopher

beside cough drops.

HEIMLICH'S BEAGLES

Heimlich (of maneuver)
and his beagles.
Die Beagles von Heimlich.
Seine Manöver mit/auf Beagles.
Sein besonderer Weg
mit ihnen.

WHO WAS DEEP BLUE

A tall, slim, black
cabinet that
required its own
hotel room when
traveling; a
grim reaper in
grand master guise
best known for its
"brute-force approach."
It's believed that
a bug in Deep
Blue's software led
to a random
(or so it seemed)
move that Kaspar-
ov mistook for
thinking (it spooked
him). A rematch?
No. No rematch.
IBM re-
tired Deep Blue, dis-

mantled it. A
lobotomy
for computers.
This successor
to Deep Thought. De-
stroyer of men.

I HAVE STUFFED MYSELF

AT DINNER

Can't even write my name
let alone the blurb you've
asked me for. I loosen my pants
and go stand alone at
the window. It is cold out,
the landscape all blue balls
and gray, and looking dead.

A glass tiger is coming
softly down to me through
dream channels, a figurine
about five inches tall
and fourteen inches long—
its tail is missing.
I think I wrote this while
on the phone with someone.
Or I had just got off the phone.
Or was about to get on.

The maître d' takes me
by the shoulders and gently
rolls me back onto the floor
like a large ball or pregnant
person, boards creaking.
I can write better than this give
me a minute.

THE BODYBUILDER

The bodyguards
guarding the body
of the bodybuilder
waited out front
in recently washed
grand-piano-black
SUVs.

He drove them
mad, taking fifty
minutes to pick out
a teacup. Holding
one, staring at it,
air sipping; holding
another, in different
light, air sipping,
cocking his head.

CHRISTMAS

It's midnight and huge white rabbits
zigzag the snow-packed road.
I shock them along with my high beams.
In my mind I've lowered my window
and am thumping the outside of my door
with a ball bat. In my mind I recklessly
cut the cookie with the cheese knife.
What do white rabbits eat, I wonder.
And do they ever sleep, I wonder.
I had a problem and I solved it.
How I solved it is none of your business.

WHO WAS GENGHIS KHAN

A tense man who
drew his eyebrows
on with ballpoint,
wet his pants a
lot, suffered pre-
mature ejac-
ulations, could
not control his
thoughts. It's said he
read poetry.
It's said he wore
pink burlap, could
stare directly
into the sun,
went sometimes by
Walter. *Walter.*
Kept strips of beef
jerky beneath
his horse blanket.
When his time came
he galloped right

at it. Clansmen
flicked beautiful
pale-blue buttons
at his casket.
Fires subsided.
Abated. Died
down. Meaning what?

LAWS OF NATURE

You can't step into the same river twice.
Unless it's into a rowboat, then you can do it.
It's not what you think, that the rowboat
is not technically the river so the—
or the boat keeps your foot dry or whatever.
It has something to do with the aluminum.
I think the rowboat has to be aluminum.

What goes up must come down. Really? You sure?
(*If it doesn't, and more than six hours pass, call your doctor.*)
And you can't put a square peg in a round hole.
Again I call bullshit, carefully stepping down
to put one foot into the center of the boat.
A shakiness flutters. A doubt, rising in a series
of short bursts through my body. I slowly bring
my other leg up and into the boat. The boat
flinching. The boat feeling like a tablecloth
about to be jerked out from under the plates
and the cups. They say never stand up in
a rowboat. I think about this as the boat moves
out into the current, and begins to pick up speed.

BRISKLY JERKED RUGS

At midnight a blinkered pony clopped up the winter road.
A single toon, weirdly amid twin rows of slippery elm.
I am called Honcho. Irrevocable have been my words.
I flick my fingertips violently, as if sprinkling a crowd.
The demitasse broods. Is alone. Is lonely.
I find I cannot go over to it.

The pony looked aggrieved, moved only to bossa nova
(ears perking to "Dumpling"). Flanked with trees
the road was white, and very straight. We stood
at the pie safe wanting in, some of us knocking,
while blue dream-tassels shook gently at the cuffs
of the robe of a well-meaning cad.

Bob sucked the golf ball through the garden hose, reluctantly.
Dot said she had toe-danced her entire way through college.
I had my head down, I was thinking. A hand reached casually
into my field of vision—the waiter touched my fries with his
Band-Aid. Baby chicks stepped into the clubhouse. Each one
tripped a bit on the rug's edge. No one stopped them.

Bob sucked a second golf ball through in half the time.
Dot held one of her ankles beside her head like a swan song.
The season unbuttoned itself in little burps of pink and white.
They fed the racehorse pot brownies in his stall. He ate them
thoughtfully. The jockey fondled his heavy snaffle. It rained
only over Roanoke. Which I guess is why I've asked you here.

Dimly did the children understand us. Still we swam at them.
Was the steeple bathed in champagne light, or exuding it?
Dale after dale after dale she said; the new priest listened
without comment. A Bundt cake was sliced at thoughtlessly.
Blind Weimaraners gently coughed on tasseled cushions.
A double entendre followed me into the coatroom.

It was unexpected, how subtly they backed the rowboat from us.
The steeple tore a mellow hole for itself in the sleeve of evening,
From fifth-floor windows came several fits of confetti.
(Almost imperceptible, the movement of the oars.)
Hair carefully combed, then tousled. Then combed again.
Then tousled.

It is autumn and another apostle has blown into town.
The public pool has been drained, its cracked bottom
not as blue as we remembered. Our peace pipes grown
so heavy with baggage. Can in fact barely lift mine.
But finally manage to swing it. You throw your back out
swinging yours, saying you'll knock my face in, laughing.

No one can see past the new apostle's chapped lips.
Due to such a violent draining we lost a few children.
Yesterday's belting left Bruce gumming his gazpacho,
a second bowl of it skidding past me at the lunch counter.
I retrace my steps, smelling shampoo on the meter maid.
The collie's mood darkens. It is not fond of walnuts.

Someone had placed some bok choy on the counter top.
The room was dark and cold and quiet.
I'd come in, flicked the lights on, turned up the heat,
and there it was. But I am paid to say nothing, this
opéra bouffe a bit weedy at the edges. An umbrella
passes blackly, out from one cab, into another.

Now here was a vegetable that would not take it anymore.
The room was dark and cold because it was a morgue
Despite good intentions we grow phonier and phonier
said the gigolo, stepping carefully from swim trunks.
Two empty canoes bombed expertly the rapids.
Turning lazily, the falcon—pretending to be deaf.

She'd called me a condiment, plainly. She meant it.
A used condom floated down the Elbe for weeks, making
no wrong moves. What exactly's my job here?
Autumn leaves move mysteriously up the center of the street.
The picnic is full of rules. Of holes.
What, exactly, is my job here?

She called me a condiment; it just rolled off her tongue.
With nothing left to lose the condom navigated the Elbe.
The waiter pulled my tie so hard I coughed.
There was a sadness in my chained bicycle—
a rainsquall had wetted it—
its private parts sparkled in lamplight.

We could smell the door prize through its protective covering.
The straining wastrel popped both his sutures and catheter.
Out over the meadow a dustpan had been flung—it circled back
like a boomerang. I'd been told my feelings were measurable.
You professed to know the Japan wax, when in fact you did not.
Opposing doxologies spun like tops on the table.

The door prize was heavy, and wet, and came from Stuttgart.
The wastrel's girlfriend Kansas Beth, also a wastrel.
August: a silver tape deck glinted in the sun. Just looking at
the gashouse made us groggy. A rangy calmness surrounded
the crown. My mood moved into the room as an elephant,
knees creaking. Somehow its tusks remained jocose.

The caterpillar chewed with its mouth open.
I said ignore the dickcissel screamed Penny.
All winter the biopsy traveled by oxcart. Repeatedly
upon a patch of bark the sunlight stroked itself.
Three days we looked for a crouton in the canebrake.
Within minutes the pet lamb ransacked the terrarium.

The caterpillar, its head back, let out a human sound.
We stood trying not to look at the dickcissel.
The accountant's buttocks spoke for themselves,
it would have been weird if they hadn't.
Passively did the cuckold shake his flower cluster.
The vibrating bottles clinked and jingled during transport.

He gently used a knuckle to adjust the glasses on his nose.
A shingle floated, unusually, past my canoe.
I understood immediately your dark beret.
The shrubbery shook at the edge of the barbecue.
We ripped apart a sock drawer looking for socks.
A beautiful chime rang once throughout the universe.

He roughly used a pickle to knock some ashes from a rose.
The shingle floated downstream faster than the current.
Fuchsias clashed with hydrangeas which choked the myrtle.
Everyone gossiped at once, no one really listening to anyone.
Two turtles reared up upon greeting.
The corn chips were wet, had been rained on, so yeah.

The candle loaned its halo to Duchamp.
White petals brushed Dawn's handbag in Berlin.
Mauve leggings found me in a thoughtful trance.
Dislodged regrets crept back into their lodge.
Peculiar feelings ripple through my hand.
Camellias bloated on the baby grand.

Duchamp regaled the candle like a champ.
Dawn swung her handbag at a passing finch.
With teen malaise the arguments ensued.
Dark pitchers slosh (head nurse leans back and burps).
Throughout the woods you smell the carrot stew.
A growing pebble, somewhere in my shoe.

I sat on the edge of the bathtub, feeling extorted.
The Percheron carefully worked his lips, loosening his tether.
A screech owl stepped quietly through the courtyard.
I'd completed law school using nothing but body language.
It seemed a cipher separated the piglets from their mothers.
In the past it was primarily vents that were made out of denim.

I went over and sat on the toilet, feeling no different.
A time when Percherons were still tied to the sides of churches
A woman named Sue worked the guillotine—an ordinary
hairpin fell through centuries from the side of her head.
We could see now how the mountain was composed of fine print.
Assumptive was what *you* said; I did not say assumptive.

He felt challenged by the fuckwad.
The nozzle was pink, was hard, was French.
The field was full of buttonwoods and ginkgos.
She arrived in a wet car the color of celery.
In the obituary the unicorns played a major role.
Mom's espousal made her gums bleed. For example

the wadfuck with his easel in the wheat field.
The nozzle reared back when we reached for it.
During *Jaws* we snacked, we prayed, we screwed.
The dwarf said he'd genuflect, but not join the Lollipop Guild.
A blue puddle was forming, even the blind man could see it.
Plot thickened—we clogged. Plot thinned—continued clogging.

I happen to be watching a sidewalk when a cornflower breaks through.
As the rain stopped a cooling croissant came into the room.
The deaf kitten had that look on its face as it chewed. Elizabeth
behaved badly, drop-kicking bags of mulch into the Volvo.
Prague stank on its hillside. We briskly jerked our rugs
to reveal moss. The feeling of winter in my mustache.

It took the cornflower seven years to get through to my smoke break.
The croissant looked funereal on its zinc tray under lamplight.
Thoughts of dead relatives moved through me like carousel horses.
A man with tremendous earlobes shovels skin at the skin farm.
Although it seems unlikely, it *is* happening. Another of
the didactic metaphors you've been running from all your life.

The thespian's patter evinced volumes.
As I watch this snowbank, an orange disappears
noiselessly into it. First Punch and then Judy
follow me jerkily into the outhouse. You note futile
puerilities. Then puerile futilities. I'm having a
shrinking feeling. A series of them, actually.

The patter gently loosened our fillings.
As I continue to watch this snowbank, a second orange
more violently follows. The sensation of dancing
passes like a parade float. A shoehorn, brooding
on the bedspread. Compulsively a midwife
breaks into impersonations of famous politicians.

The physician was frank. His nose was red and large.
Scientists had discovered nerve endings in a manure pile.
Just the very tip of a barren tree branch tapped occasionally
on the study window. Joy said there was a rupture in her
maple bar, pointing to a hairline crack in its surface.
Hans had to stroke a cat in order to write a poem.

To the physician his beer can felt open, cold, and heavy.
The manure pile emitted a steady, uninterrupted moan
I will play *the wet cat*, you will come at me with a towel.
There will be an idling car, windows partially fogged.
Horses will approach, first one and then another, to try
looking in, big eyes scanning for Betsy.

The casket had been painted to look like a thesaurus.
Gamers gathered at the grocery to watch the unloading of produce.
Tam set poached eggs on the counter, along with an affidavit
and bacon. I carefully unwrapped another cube of bubble gum.
I was having a conversation with the leaves of a bush.
The repairman felt puny; he knelt on burgundy mud flaps.

The casket had been thumped on and sounded quite canorous.
The gamers had never seen a real can of cat food before.
The simplest sentence involving lumber was what I was after.
    d-dah d-dah . . . d-dah d-dah . . .
d-dah d-dah d-dah-dah . . . The five types of men's faces
were being painted on the side of the pharmacy.

The forest was full of chainsaws, and Dutch men in swim thongs.
The choir looked ashen; they sang in earnest of eternity.
At the edge of the snow I encountered a bag of tangerines.
To cuddle now seems disingenuous, observed Lorna, swatting at a fly
with a rubber ruler. Jessie shook his bangs like a pony, dumping Splenda
into his breve. He nodded, and murmured, and listened to Lorna.

The forest smelled of gasoline. And mushrooms. And coconut oil.
The choir looked startled, belting out "Blessed Assurance" with bluster.
A limping child could be heard dragging her knuckles in the hallway.
A holiday wind ascended the glen, whatever that meant.
We'd turned over a new leaf as they say. Words of atonement
moving low and cold like propane through the orchard.

A scrawny dream began to flow.
Man attempts to hang self with tea towel.
The mint lozenge had traveled from Auckland.
I held onto the banister with both hands
as you pulled my socks off. Sausage thunder
shook the hostel. Feed only Pepsi to a gerbil.

A scrawny dream flowed right and left.
The tea towel sat all humpty on the counter.
Men came to swap the mattresses at noon.
The corridor smelled like a fresh can of tennis balls.
You reproached me with a candlesnuffer.
Unshakable sadness as I entered the oven mitt.

Some vulgar conversation was coming from the hedge.
I stood in the garage a long time, washing the punching bag.
The runaway horse came back; he let himself into the yard
latching the gate behind him. A barber called Carl ran
a finger through pollen on the hood of the hearse.
A tinted window opened one inch, briefly. Then closed.

Some vulgar conversation blew delicately in from Alabama.
Throughout the seventies all punching bags were carefully stuffed
with daisies at the factory. Knowing what I know now it's hard
to pretend I know less. Or more. A nut-bearing tree elicits
mixed reviews. A blue hatchet waits for spring. Sister Helen
unslams the rectory door, looking refreshed.

The eulogy felt tidy but broken. Still you delivered it.
The stockman was reticent, loved even his hay fever.
For some reason I'd put my knee up to the peephole.
A volley of candied patter issued forth without warning.
The asininity surprised Barb. Her husband the brow-
beaten. (He pole danced for pocket change.)

The eulogy rolled over like a fat baby we cared a lot about.
The stockman tipped his hat back, used the word *ambrosia*
twice in ten minutes. Sissy tossed a salad so hard her
wrists hurt. Into one another certain sounds clinked
nicely. I am approaching a stranger's bed in the dark,
to lay my heavy coat on a pile of heavy coats.

NOTES

HOW TO FIX A BROKEN BUTTERFLY WING is for Alice Neild and takes its title from a YouTube video of the same name.

TOWN was written for the anthology *Unearthing Paradise*, a collection of prose and poetry protesting a proposed gold mine in Montana's Paradise Valley.

CHUNK OF SEA GLASS is for Joe Fletcher.

WHO WAS THE SUN was written in response to a painting by Bozeman artist Jay Schmidt.

THIS LOOKS RUSSIAN TO ME: The painting described here is *A Drowned Woman* by Vasily Perov (1867).

WHAT BUGGED ME WAS was inspired by Man Ray's photograph of the dead Marcel Proust.

SOME TEA HAS EVAPORATED HERE is for Tyler Meeks.

YOUR PAINTING was written in response to the painting *Spring of Life* by Scott Simler, for an art project organized by Zachary Schomburg and Therese Heitkamp of the Stark County Board of Developmental Disabilities in Canton, Ohio—in partnership with The Workshops, Inc.

GENTLY TAPPING RAVIOLIS IN A POT
OF BOILING WATER is for Jono Tosch.

THE BRANCHES OF CLOWNS is for Adrian Kien.

THE SIGNAL was written with Chris Murray,
trading lines via text messages.

28 APRIL 2016 is for Tyler Meeks.

ACKNOWLEDGMENTS

Grateful acknowledgment is made to the editors
and staff of the following magazines/journals
where many of these poems originally appeared:

Big Sky Journal ∗ *Columbia Journal* ∗ *Gulf Coast Online*
jubilat ∗ *Logue* (2015) ∗ *The New Yorker*
New York Tyrant ∗ *Pouch* ∗ *The Volta*

Many thanks to Aaron Parrett of the Territorial Press
in Helena, Montana, for his broadside of "Christmas."

"The Couple" appeared in the anthology *Privacy Policy:
The Anthology of Surveillance Poetics*, edited by Andrew Ridker.

"Town" appeared in the anthology *Unearthing Paradise*, edited
by Marc Beaudin, Seabring Davis, and Max Hjortsberg.

Thanks to Kelly Dick, Greg Keeler, and Susan Thomas
for reading an early draft of this book and giving
valuable feedback. And special thanks to Matthew
Zapruder who looked carefully at later drafts.

And finally I want to thank everyone at Wave Books
for their meticulous work, insights, patience,
and support. I feel lucky to know them.